The
Cosmic Gardener

Andrew Ableton

DEDICATION

This book is dedicated to the Powers that Be.

CONTENTS

THE COSMIC GARDENER

ACKNOWLEDGMENTS

My Beautiful, Amazing Wife,

And, my Precious Family.

Strip the meat from the bone,

And ask for nothing,

As we have nothing,

We have, absolutely that that we were given when we came,

And, what we take when we go.

Introduction

Thank you for taking the time to read this collection of some of the most precious and personal spiritual experiences that span 50 years of my life. Each one of the following chapters will give you a personal account of my journey along with some unique perspectives of what happened to me from the young age of 5 years old. These wonderful and personally enriching experiences are only part of my journey and are highlighted here to provide you with a flavour and some colour of what has happened to me over the years of my life. I believe that I have been so fortunate to have many, many more wonderful and dramatic experiences than the ones that I have shared with you in this book, each year a new teaching, a new spiritual awakening. It has truly been a blessed life that I have lived thus far and I thank the God's for these deep and wonderful spiritual connections, profound experiences and life changing teachings. This journey has been deeply personal and soul searching, it has brought many moments of profound excitement and sadness. It has provided me with a unique take on life, and a journey of solitude and deep understanding of the interconnectivity of the physical and the spiritual realms. Ultimately, this journey has

2

revealed to me our true purpose in this life, 'the meaning of life' as we call it. One that we have all searched for at one time or another in our lives.

My connections and experiences did not come to me by my choice, nor did they come through any person that is living, each and every experience was initiated through differing spirit forces, all connected to one source, individually unique in their construct and output. My journey led me through Christianity as a child, in to spirituality as a young man, through the wonders of Islam, and finally in to a special place that has no label or following.

The following chapters traverse the 50 years of my life and they terminate with the most dramatic, deep and powerful teaching of them all, the meaning of life, our purpose and our journey, the Cosmic Gardener.

I hope that you find something in this book that connects and resonates with your personal growth and spiritual awakening, providing you with comfort, joy, happiness, curiosity and maybe a few life enriching lessons on the way.

THE COSMIC GARDENER

1 ALL OR NOTHING

Acceptance without delay is negating the mindset, furthering and consequence with hurried consent.

I was young, and energetic, a curious 5 years old boy, growing up in the North West of England, the year was 1975. I lived with my mother, father and older sister in a cosy terraced, stone cottage in the centre of a small sleepy village. The cottage had 2 small bedrooms and a small back garden with an outside toilet. Adjacent to the back garden lay open land, this area had once existed as a narrowboat canal, a waterway that had once carried canal barges, bringing coal and other supplies in to Lancashire many years earlier. The canal had been filled in and covered over a long time ago, over grown with trees, bushes and weeds, the canal had been returned to nature. The area was quiet most of the time with the infrequent dog walker and young couples passing by. As an adventurous 5 year old I frequently spent my free time playing there in solitude, exploring the undergrowth for whatever I might find. It was late April, a Sunday and late afternoon, the sky was grey with thick cloud, and a light breeze pushed the clouds slowly across the sky, I was out playing alone as usual, and had decided to climb one of the large tree that hung over the canal. The tree was very close to the garden fence which was parted with a small gate that divided the garden from the open land. I had climbed this particular tree many times before and I knew automatically where to place my feet and hands to climb without falling, confidently raising myself as high as I possibly could to the highest most branches of the tree. I concentrated my efforts and carefully climbed, and within a moment I was swaying in the light breeze, gripping tightly to the green smooth flexible branches that pointed skyward at the top of the tree. I felt the sway and bend of the branches and stopped, as to go any further or higher was dangerous and I knew very well that I should not climb too high. My mother's voice whispered in my ear, "not too high, be careful," As my focus shifted from climbing to securing my position, I sat back against a twisted branch and adjusted my feet to be sure that I was not going to fall. My attention was drawn to a small bird to the left of me that had caught my gaze. I twisted my body to get a better view and re-adjusted my footing, as I stared at the bird I realised that it had somehow got caught up in the branch of the tree and was suspended upside down, its' leg was broken and trapped. I stared at the poor little bird and the bird stared back at me, I felt shocked and bothered, not knowing what to do. The little bird hardly moved, it made no sound and as I focused more and more, the world seemed to phase out and stop, everything had frozen in that very brief moment. Within that quiet and empty space a sudden and overwhelming rush of emotion and sadness filled my heart, it burned and felt painful in my chest, my breath shortened and quickened, my muscles tensed, and suddenly, without warning I felt something move from deep inside my body, a shift of some kind, like my shadow moving across the pavement as I walked along. Something moved from inside me to the outside of my body, it was still part of me, still attached somehow but separate in some way, a new feeling that I did not understand, it vibrated and expanded, it swelled and rushed out of my very being, it intensified and I felt a dramatic connection, a connection to everything in the Universe, it was big and it expanded outward, it felt as though I was at one with everything that existed in the Universe and beyond, everything that had existed in the past and everything that will exist in the future. An unstoppable energy coursed through me and out of me, every molecule of my small young body pulsated and vibrated, I felt alive, like I had never felt before, it was exquisite, a brief but significant life changing moment, a moment that I would cherish, one that would never leave me for the rest of my life, the beginning of a wonderful and special journey, a profound and unique connection. Nothing like this had happened to me before, nothing had prepared me for this significant and dramatic experience, my first out of body and deeply spiritual awakening. Up to this point in my short existence, I had been just another 5 year old in the world, growing and experiencing my life with my family and friends, understanding the basic concepts of my surroundings.

For a brief moment in time I had connected to something indescribable, something mysterious and exquisite, it was as though a surge of energy had pushed out from my very core and connected me to everything, the known and the unknown, a total, sudden and all-consuming connection.

The moment passed as quickly as it came, the feeling, the energy, the pause in time, it was completely gone. I breathed deeply, refocusing my gaze back to the poor little bird, still motionless, upside down and trapped, hanging from the tree. I carefully freed the little bird, gently moving its tiny leg from the branch and carefully cradling it in my right hand, I made my way down from the tree and back in to my garden. I quickly found a small box in my fathers shed and carefully and slowly placed the bird inside, cushioned on some old towelling. I ran inside quickly and told my mother what had happened to the bird and what had happened to it in the tree. I did not tell her about my experience with the energy and the connection that had briefly and dramatically affected me, it felt personal and special and I did not want to talk about it to anyone. Sadly the bird did not live for very long and passed away later that same day. I was consumed and filled with sadness, not for the bird, but for the depth of the emptiness that now lived within me, the sudden and total disconnection from the energy that had very briefly flooded through me and out of me earlier that day, nothing now felt the same as it was before, life had now changed, it would never return to where I was before the experience. I felt an emotion that ached to my core, every breath was another second of an existence without connection, without life.

My mother had noticed this change and tried to comfort me with supportive words about the bird and the fact that I had tried to save it and I should not be sad. My mother was unaware of the true reason that my sadness was inconsolable, and no words of comfort would stop the heartache.

In the weeks that followed I sat in the same tree as many times as I could, resting against the same bent branch, securing my feet in the same way as before, sat with my eyes closed and feeling the sway of the tree as the wind moved me backwards and forwards, waiting and hoping for something to happen, waiting for that all-consuming connection. Time after time I climbed that tree, waiting and hoping, desperately for something. There was nothing, nothing happened, nothing moved in my core, no energy, no connection, no life. I felt profound sadness, and totally alone, it was inescapable. The connection had brought with it something else, a connection to someone or something that I now could not feel and no longer had with me, and certainly did not understand, I felt totally alone in the world, I went to sleep feeling the same as I did when I woke, every day, desperately alone, with one mission, to find whatever it was and connect with it again for as long as I could and for as many times as I could.

I sat in many trees and bushes in the weeks and months that followed, hoping and wishing for something, and still no connection came.

I attended the local primary school every day during the week, the school was small and had a large tarmacked playground surrounded by fields and trees, it was the area that all the children would congregate in and would play there at break times and during their lunch hour. It was a Wednesday afternoon and all the children were outside playing, it was break time and it had been raining. The rain had briefly stopped and the ground was still wet, rain water had accumulated at the edge of the playground in the soil depressions and spaces between the tarmac and the grass. The rain water that had collected in the depression between the playground and the field was clear and approximately 10 cm deep. I still felt the deep sadness and an alone feeling that I just could not shake off, nothing seemed to fit anymore, and life had certainly changed. I stood gazing in to the water at the edge of the playground, children were happily playing in the background and I could hear the noise of their voices as they joyfully ran round. I reached in to the pocket of my jacket and pulled out the small toy figure of a soldier, I had found it sometime ago whilst playing along the canal close to home. I stared into the water at the edge of the playground and dropped the figure in to it, the figure sank slowly to the bottom, resting face up on the submerged grass. I stared at the figure, the water was clear and I could see the detail of the soldiers face, its army uniform and its black shinny boots. I stared and focused on the soldier's features, my mind drifted and again the connection came, suddenly and without warning. I felt the same shift from inside my core, an expansion of energy and a connection to everything, I felt warm and alive, it felt like I had waited a life time for this moment, life had returned. This time the connection was different, the energy felt the same as before but there was also a presence, I was now not alone, someone or something was stood with me, standing close behind me, it was not physical, not a person or another child in the playground, I could feel its presence, it stood taller than me, and it was also staring down at the figure in the water. I froze, I couldn't move, I did not look round, I just focused my eyes on the figure of the soldier submerged in the water. Whatever it was that was stood with me brought a secure and warm feeling, and I glowed in the energy that now flowed through me. The figure impressed a feeling on me, an awareness, a deep and meaningful understanding, it did not speak, it did not make a sound and did not physically touch me. It was the space, the space between the physical world and the spiritual, a divide that was as real as the water that was between the soldier and the playground. The soldier was me and the water was the divide, on the other side of the divide was the entity, it felt close, it was close enough to touch, but at the same time it was as far away as the sun. The figure moved in closer behind me and the energy flow increased, the energy that was now flowing through me was intertwined with that of the entity, it felt like liquid silver, a river of molten energy, an experience without words or thoughts that could explain or describe the significance of this experience, a seed had been planted deep in my heart, one that would grow with every breath that I would take for the rest of my life. This was my second precious connection, and again it ended as quickly as it had begun.

Although this second experience and connection was brief, the understanding was burned and imprinted in to my memory, in to my very soul. I left the toy soldier submerged in the water and walked slowly backwards to the centre of the playground until I could no longer see the soldier. Tears welled up in my eyes and ran down my face, the feeling of disconnection and of being totally alone again filled my heart and saddened me deeply. I was confused, and could feel opposing forces conflicting deep within my emotion, a light had now been shone in the darkness, a spark, an ignition for growth that pushed at the sadness, and brought a comfort that I had not felt before, I breathed deeply and cleared my thoughts. Children were still playing, running, jumping, shouting, pushing and yelling in the playground, but the alone feeling remained, where had the connection gone, why was it gone, how do I bring it back? The break time whistle blew and all the children moved busily back in to the school.

Uncover the order for chaos,

Ring true the bells of change aloft,

Without the chaos the bells ring true.

2 THE BEGINNING

As with the end the new beginning will come,

As before the more,

Accept the key and breathe,

For all you see is where we will be.

Ask for a reason and not for the time,

Time is forgiving and quick to the end.

THE COSMIC GARDENER

See all the glory of all that is,

Through time is provided.

Amass these words and provide your shelter,

As strong and robust,

For all, insist and speak these words,

From high and long,

Through big and small,

Provide, provide, provide.

Years had now passed and I, my mother and sister had moved house, we had moved closer to my Grandparents house as my mother and father had now divorced, my mother had remarried and I was now 8 years old, a new school, a new place to live. The new house was bigger and newer than the last house, I had my own bedroom and the house had a front and rear garden and an inside toilet. A new school to attend, a new start.

The new house was within 2 miles of the local river, a place that I would find solace and connection with nature. The new school was similar to the old school, small and located within the countryside, over time I made new friends, and there was a similarity to this place as my previous home and surroundings. Still feeling alone and searching for connection, I hadn't lost the experience, it had not diminished with the years that had passed, it was engrained within me and I knew that I would carry what felt like a heavy burden for the rest of my life.

My closeness to my grandfather grew, he was a charismatic, story teller, a real and authentic character, self-styled, brimming with stories from the Second World War and from his own childhood, growing up in Oldham. My grandfather owned and ran an antiques business in the nearest town, he was a qualified watch and clock maker and repairer and he dripped in yellow gold. A large golden lion with sapphire eyes hung from a heavy chain around his neck, a gold pocket watch sat in the breast pocket of his waistcoat, again on a heavy chain, he also wore 2 heavy gold rings, one was a full gold sovereign and the other a diamond ring that he had made by his own hand. I would sit listening to my grandfather's stories for hours, periodically observing my grandfather attire. The gold jewellery was interesting and larger than life, but the one thing that I would focus on every time I visited my Grandad was the large pipe that he constantly smoked, bellowing thick grey sweet liquorice smoke in to the room every few minutes. In between stories his pipe would burn out and he would relight it with a match from his ornate match box that had his name engraved on the copper shinny cover. Within these moments with my grandfather I would feel comfort and a lessening of the ache that was constantly with me. I never shared my experiences with my grandfather, I did not want my relationship with him changing in any way. This time was for me and my Grandad, it wasn't for the connection.

Time passed and I had moved to secondary school, I was now 14 years old and still spent many hours every week with my Grandad. I never tired of my Grandad's stories and even though many stories had been repeated, there was always something new to take away. I also spent some time with friends from school, with the majority of my time by the river in solitude. I had a few favourite trees that I frequently climbed and sat in, as I had done many years earlier. I longed for another experience, just one more chance to feel that energy pulsing through my body.

Winter was fast approaching and I was told by my mother that my father's brother was gravely ill, he had terminal cancer and he did not have long to live. The family were going to visit and I would need to come along. This was a strange and new experience for me, my uncle was frail and gaunt, he was weak and looked very poorly. I watched as my mother and stepfather uncomfortably chatted to my uncle, talking about life that soon my uncle would not have. The visit was soon over and the family returned home.

Two weeks had passed after seeing my uncle, I was in my bedroom and it was a school night, I was busily completing my homework. As I concentrated on the maths questions that had been set, I felt a shiver down my spine, a brief wave of energy passed through me and I slowly put my books down. I closed my eyes and concentrated, was this it, after all this time, has it returned, nothing came, 5 minutes, 10 minutes, still nothing. I went back to my homework and eventually readied myself for bed. Again the wave of energy passed through me, it was from the same direction as the first wave, and this time I watched as the shimmering energy passed through my bedroom window as it left me. This was it I thought, it was back, colour filled the room, life had finally returned.

Again, I concentrated and nothing came, 5 minutes, 10 minutes and then there it was again, slower and stronger, it passed through me and through the window. I lay in bed, wide eyed, waiting and hoping. I had waited almost an hour and was close to falling asleep when I was abruptly brought to my senses by a figure that had suddenly appeared in the small bedroom, it was a man, a tall man, stood within a few feet of my bed looking down at me. It was my uncle, the man that was gravely ill that I had visited 2 weeks earlier. I could see his facial features, he wasn't ill and looked the same as I had remembered him before his illness. He looked down at me and our eyes fixed, I could feel my heart pounding but I still felt a calmness, there was nothing said, no information, just a presence that was unmistakably my uncle that was now very poorly. My uncle's figure began to fade and at the moment that the figure evaporated my uncle gestured, pointed upwards. I sat awake for a time, replaying the experience over and over, and eventually dropping to sleep. I was awoken by a movement in my room, it was still dark and the house was quiet, again my uncle had appeared, this time he was not stood over me, he was floating above the bed looking down. This was a shock but I still felt calm and comfortable, again my uncle pointed upwards and evaporated. Again I slept and was awoken by something in my room, again my uncle, but this time it was just his torso that was visible. At the very second that my uncle evaporated and left, the energy that I had been waiting for, for all these years was with me, the energy filled me and flowed through me, the entity was back and brought a message, clear and concise, "Your uncle has passed on, he has crossed the divide", these words were not spoken or heard, they were pushed in to my physical being. This information came with a strong feeling, an overwhelming emotion, elation, a release, a celebration, a return home for my uncle, a return to source, the one, a return to the entity, a release of time, a release of struggle, of pain, of worldly anchors. My uncle was returned to where he had begun. Again the connection ended quickly

21

and after some time I dropped back to sleep.

I desperately wanted to speak to my mother about my experience, I wanted to shout it out so everyone everywhere could hear it, it was life and it was everything. I hurried downstairs in the morning, bursting with my experience, desperate to tell my mother all about my uncle and his passing. As I walked in to the kitchen where my mother was making breakfast, I slowed and started to feel anxious, my heart raced and a fear came over me. I stared at my mother and quickly diverted my eyes, a moment ago I was desperate to tell her every detail of my experience, and now nothing, I had nothing to say. I looked up again at my mother who was standing by the cooker, I could see the anchors that held her down to the earth, the same anchors that my uncle had released as he left, I felt my mother's emotion, the chains and locks that tied her to life. I stepped back and was about to leave the room but my mother had already noticed me. "Are you OK" she asked, "Yes, thanks'" I replied, "all good." My mother stared at me waiting for more, more conversation, I smiled uneasily and stepped forward, taking a slice of bread from the bread package and placing it in the toaster. I made small talk with my mother until she had finished making breakfast. My sister had luckily walked in and took the focus away from me, I slipped away quietly and readied myself for school.

Returning home that night I was met at the door by my mother, "bad news' she said, it's your uncle", he had passed away in the night, "It was a good passing" she said. If only she had known how amazing it was and how beautiful his passing had actually been.

A few days had passed and I was told that we were to go to our uncle's funeral, this was my first funeral, another new experience.

The day of the funeral came and my uncle was to be cremated, my uncle's family, work colleagues and friends attended the funeral. My aunty and cousins met us at the crematorium entrance, I had no words to speak to them with, I just smiled respectfully and put my head down as I moved quickly to my seat. The service was relatively quick and the coffin disappeared behind a motorised curtain, there was sadness and heartache, it was a difficult experience, especially as I felt the opposite, joy and happiness for my uncle and his passing. As the music played and the vicar spoke, I felt a deep pain in my chest, it was the terrible pain that was being felt by my close family at the passing of my uncle, the complete loss of a husband, a father, a son. I felt it, deep in my soul, it was hot like the sun, it burned and twisted my gut. The funeral service closed and the group moved outside in to the grounds of the crematorium. My emotions overflowed, I sobbed uncontrollably and tears streamed from my eyes, my mother put her hand on me to comfort me, "It's OK," she said, "Your uncle is in a better place." I fought back the tears, looked in to my mother's eyes and whispered, "It's not for him, it's for them, their pain, their loss, they don't know where he has gone, they just don't know how lucky he is." My mother looked at me confused and complexed for a moment as my words were not what she was expecting to hear. She paused for a moment and then continued to speak to other family members, pushing past my words. This had been an important lesson for me, now I understood how lost and disconnected people can be in the world, unsure of the future, anchored to life and the inevitable life events that would eventually release everyone as it had my uncle. I felt this special moment, it was a seed that would grow inside me, one that would give me a life in the world, unique and open to whatever was to come my way.

3 ETERNAL GROWTH

Postulate frankly deep wounds to expel,

Leave open and flayed,

For these are the journey,

The flower the petals the stamen complete

The cycle the circle.

No beginning no end the whole and the nothing,

Grow and expand.

THE COSMIC GARDENER

Live, honour the life that is the gift of many,

The weathering and the storm,

The deepest yet finest,

The bright and the dull forever intern.

Join hands for connection,

Hold fear and distain

The flow is abound us,

Forever remain.

I was now 16 years of age, I had left school and was now working as an apprentice engineer. A connection had grown within me, a space had opened up within my mind's eye that was surrounded by darkness, beyond the darkness was the connection. This was the void, the space between all living things, time and space and then beyond this space was everything else, eternal, glorious connection, without limit, without time. The darkness would periodically be disturbed by movement, by figures that would move in and out of the dark space, not enough to discern who or what they were but just enough to be noticed, this continued for a few months until a sudden and dramatic appearance came out of the darkness. A large and quite fierce looking black muscular bull that moved menacingly backwards and forwards in this space, in and out of the darkness, making its presence and mood known every time it stepped forward. It would stare at me and snort, putting its head down, walking up and down, stopping only to raise its head and stare again. I felt that there was something wrong, that I had done, or was doing something wrong, the bull was a sign, a sign of frustration from the connection. This bothered me, I worried that I was not doing something that I should be doing, I worried and constantly spoke to the connection, asking for information, an explanation, but nothing came forth.

I slowly but surely became acceptant of the bull and it's gesturing, I had resigned myself to the reality of his new connection and mind's eye view.

One morning I awoke to an empty space in my mind's eye, the bull had gone, this was not abnormal, the bull would come and go, there was no pattern. I sat in the kitchen eating my breakfast and talking with my family. A movement came from the darkness, ahh the bull, I thought, a swish of movement from the darkness, another swish and then, not the bull, but something else. This was bigger, a large Buffalo stepped forward. Although the Buffalo was clearly a different animal to the Bull, it was the same entity. The bull and the buffalo were the same, its eyes and its movements were exactly the same. It moved backwards and forwards, snorting and stomping. The difference was the energy that the Buffalo brought, softer and wiser, this was a different animal with different energy.

I was now expecting a few months of the Buffalo and then maybe a different animal. I had become quite accustomed to this large companion.

The Buffalo had been with me for a couple of days and I was walking alone by the river, a forceful energy came from nowhere and pushed at me from the back. It pushed at me to the point of falling forward but I was physically not moving, something inside me was moving forward every time the energy pushed. Again the energy pushed at me and part of me fell forward and out. Part of me, part of my energy, my soul, my spirit was now part in part out of my body. I could sense and feel the connection. The energy shift had connected me across the darkness and in to the connection. I sat down under a tree to try and understand these new feelings and situation. As I sat down my mind, my senses shifted into the connection, I was now in a new world, a totally different space and time that my physical was in. As my senses cleared I realised that I was not alone in this spiritual space, I was in a small enclosed area and was not alone, I could hear a drum rhythmically beating and some form of chanting but could not see anything. A thick steam filled the space and it was hot, very hot. The drumming and chanting increased in intensity, a brief moment of pressure pushed out from my energy and then pop, I was flying above the trees. I could see mountains and forest, I was flying, I was an eagle, I felt my wing feathers as they adjusted to the slightest wind change. I was an eagle soaring above the trees, free and alive. I could still hear the chanting and drumming, I still knew that I was sat under the tree by the river but this, this feeling of flying and being free was the most amazing feeling, I swooped and I climbed, I felt the sun warming my body through my feathers. As I climbed again, adjusting my wing position to compensate for the wind pocket that I was using to rise, pop, again I was back, enveloped in the steam. I could now see the others sat with me, they were all men, four of them, not English but Indian, American Indian. They chanted and stared at me, they could see me as clearly as I could see them. The shift came again and I was back in my body, sat under the tree by the river. All had returned to normal, I was back and the Buffalo was there again. I rushed home and decided to explore the local library to see what information I could find out about American Indians. I found information about American Indian sweat lodges and spirit animals, the way of the shaman, but the information that I had found was limited and did not explain any of these new experiences.

I became frustrated and thirsty for more information and more experiences. I waited and waited, I sat, I walked, I slept, consumed by this most recent experience. It was another 2 week before I had a further connection and experience. Again, an energy pushed at me from the back and my spirit, soul, whatever it was moved out and connected across the darkness in to the connection. This time, I was sat in an open space, one older man sat in front of me, cross legged, as though he had been waiting for my arrival. I stared at the man, he was American Indian, he had long grey hair that was platted, with dark bird feathers sticking out from the back of his hair. In front of him was a circle of stones intersected with a stone cross, I stared inquisitively at it and looked back at the man sat in front of me. The man looked at me and nodded as to acknowledge what the circle was. The man raised his arm and pointed his finger towards the centre of the circle, I was instantly raised up above the circle approximately 30 feet in to the air. The man was still pointing at the circle and as he pointed to different quadrants of the circle I spun like a compass needle. The man was talking and imparting information, I could hear him but could understand nothing that was being said. As the man moved his hand from quadrant to quadrant I would spin like the compass needle again and again. Eventually the man stopped talking, he stopped pointing and I was instantly sat back in front of him. The man's face showed concern, he stared at me, this was a wise man, he had knowledge of the connection, he lived with it, and he knew it intimately. He gestured to me to leave and instantly I was back in my body. Again I went eagerly to the library to try and find some information that would explain this experience. The man had shown me a wheel, a medicine wheel. I found lots of information about this wheel and the American Indian understanding of it, but, there was nothing about the movement, nothing that explained the experience, only that the wheel represented the four directions and somehow represented the body, spirit, intellect and lots of other things that I found confusing. This further experience had certainly set me on a journey, a quest for all things American Indian, I read, I thought and pondered and finally felt that I was on a path, a worthy journey.

Another few weeks had passed and the Buffalo had become my constant companion. The Buffalos actions had changed, it was now lethargic and would sit in the dark space for hours, stand and walk off slowly, disappearing in to the blackness. It would come and go, but its power, its energy had also changed, it was subdued, almost sleepy. The Buffalo stood again and walked in to the darkness, I had hardly noticed as it had been so many months that this experience had been with me. As the Buffalo disappeared in to the darkness a human arm came from the darkness, and this certainly focused my concentration. The arm waved to draw my attention, the movement was specific and measured, the arm was moving left to right in an arc, backwards and forward it moved. From the darkness came a wheel, a medicine wheel, I instantly recognised it from my earlier experience. A large wheel with a cross in the centre. As the arm moved backwards and forwards the wheel turned, I felt the shift as the wheel moved, an undulation, a feeling of lightness then heaviness, a moving in and moving out, closer to the connection and then further away. Connect, disconnect, deeper, darker, lighter. The arm moved, the wheel moved and I felt the shift deeper towards the connection and then further away back towards human light. The wheel split in to an open shape, it moved and it felt like the earth and the universe moved with it. The space between life and the connection was in this wheel, life, death, the soul, the spirit, everything was here and was being manipulated by this arm from the darkness. The man attached to the arm stepped forward, it was the man who had been sat in front of the wheel in the open ground. He had the energy of the Buffalo, the Bull, he had strength, softness, light and darkness and his very fingertips. He was controlling the space between life and death, he pushed the wheel towards me and I absorbed it in to my very soul. The man stepped back and the dark space was empty once again. I was elated, I was filled with knowledge of thousands of years of American Indian teachings. I felt the movement between darkness and light and could shift in and out of this space at will. A rich and wonderful lesson, a sacred trust between humans and the spiritual realm, handed down from generation to generation and now entrusted to me. I felt honoured and at the same time felt unworthy of such precious teachings.

THE COSMIC GARDENER

5 corners of makers more great than before,

The coming together free fallow to all.

Be ready and open be mindful and set,

The unicorn will guide you to man's true consent.

For fire and for water the East will provide,

The young and the older, voracious and mild.

For Earth and the heavens the West will set free

Nobody will suffer just learn how to be.

The North and the South will connect the divine,

No lower or upper just centre define.

No rules, no engagement in man's holy quest,

This function and action to end for the rest,

Serene breath before motion, clear thought before all,

Give way to temptation turn many to all.

Rebuke, admonish the forsaken and cold,

Vanquish their silence new ways to uphold.

THE COSMIC GARDENER

4 A FURTHER UNDERSTNDING

I was now 18, I had recently passed my driving test and I had purchased my first car. When I could I spent my nights visiting friends in the local town, frequenting the bars and socialising, I was a happy and energetic young man and life was full of opportunity. I was now looking for more, I wanted to meet new people and find others like me, I wanted to surround myself with people who had similar experiences, ones that felt the same as I did.

Luckily fate had brought me a contact through a work colleague, my work colleague had a friend who was a member of a spiritualist church in the nearest city. I was certainly interested but didn't know whether or not to make contact. My experiences had become so personal and so internalised, I wasn't sure if this was the right path or whether I truly wanted to finally expose this precious life. I pushed it from my mind and continued with my life.

I was driving home late one night following a visit to my friend's house who lived in the nearest town, heavy metal music played loudly on the tape in my car, and I felt free. The road was well known to me and as an 18 year old young man I drove fast and enjoyed my time alone in my car. The road was well lit and quiet, my journey home would soon be over and I drummed my hands on the dashboard of the car in time to the music whilst singing along. Suddenly without warning an all-consuming pain drove in to my stomach, it was as though I had been impaled by a spear made of ice, it drove in to my centre and as the pain grew it spread in to my body like a toxin, I doubled up in pain and it took my breathe away. I felt a darkness swell within me, one that I had not felt before, the pain was intense and I could feel a sinister and evil presence with me in the car. The presence moved closer to me and it expressed its intention on me, it was clear and simple, you will die tonight and I will take your soul. I was truly scared, and I was fighting for my very life, I tried to resist by tensing my body, tensing my stomach muscles as to stop the spear from driving deeper in to my chest. It was futile, I knew that I had to get home as fast as I could, it was my only chance. I needed help. The pain pushed and tore at my insides, like a poisonous river flowing in to my cells, growing shards of black ice, the pain and the darkness grew. I eventually reached home, I pushed open the car door, and fell from my car on to my knees, crawling in to the house. I climbed the stairs on my knees, finally making it to my bedroom. I had passed my mother's bedroom on the way to mine, her door was open and she had noticed me moving past her door, she shouted, "Are you OK?" I mumbled and pulled myself on to the bed, life was draining from me and no matter what I did the entity continued to drain the life from me. In desperation I reached out my hand towards the ceiling and whispered "God, please help me." It was my last breath, my last hope. Before I could take my next breath a hand firmly placed itself in mine and a flood of golden light filled my body. It happened almost instantaneously, the golden light extinguished the darkness, it resonated through my cells, eradicating the death that was upon me. It was the hand of God, I had been saved, spared from a terrible end. My mother shouted again, "Is that you, what's going on, are you drunk" she barked. I instantly sat up and I was glowing with the light that had flooded in to me, tears streamed down my face and I felt totally overwhelmed. I stood and walked slowly in to my mother's bedroom. My mother looked up from her magazine, shocked and taken aback, "What on earth has happened?" I walked over to my mother to try and explain, the tears were still flooding from my eyes and the emotion was overwhelming, I was unable to speak. My mother sat forward and reached out her hand to touch me and with a profound shock she jerked backwards away from me. She looked at me, also unable to speak, I was too hot to touch, she stammered a few words and just sat there staring as I stood next to her bed crying and crying. I sat down slumping on to the bed, and my mother tried again to touch me. Again she moved her hand quickly away, "What on earth is this, what's happened, what is it?" she cried. I sat and cried, I was filled with Gods light and energy, I pulsated and it flowed and flowed. I lay down at the side of my mother and eventually slept. In the morning my mother was keen to understand what had happened the night before, her questions came quick and there were lots of them. As I opened my mouth to tell her the story, the emotion came riding up my throat and choked my words. It took three days before I could bring myself to speak about my experience, my mother looked at me with eyes that didn't understand any of my words, or believe what I was describing. I felt very uncomfortable and said that I didn't want to speak about it any further. I limited the amount of information I told my mother and it was soon brushed over. My mother never looked at me the same again, as she had done before I had told her, before she had been told something that she just could not understand. Her life anchors were shaken but certainly not shifted.

This experience had shaken me, my life was in danger, something had taken the opportunity to try and get me, to try and kill me and it was certainly winning until I had been saved. I was also concerned that my desperate call for help was answered so quickly, so suddenly, it had felt like a test, a test of faith, faith in what I had called 'God'. I was not a religious person, I had no belief, yes, I had gone to church with my parents when I was younger, but this had given me no connection, no feelings of belief or faith. I continued to worry about this new experience and now pushed myself to visit the Spiritualist Church that my work friend had mentioned.

I felt very nervous and worried about my visit to the Spiritualist Church, I wasn't sure what I would find, or what these people were doing in the church. I went on a Sunday, it felt like the best day to go, as my previous Church visits had been on Sunday's. I sat at the back of the church on a hard plastic chair, with space between myself and two others that sat in the same line. It wasn't long before I was being chatted to by the regulars that frequented the Church. This was very similar to a normal church I thought, a service, singing songs, it just was not what I was looking for. At the end of the service I stood up quickly, ready to leave and was approached by a middle aged woman who asked me whether I knew what Reiki Healing was. I looked confused and said no, the woman drew symbols on the palm of her hand with a finger from her other hand, I can feel the energy activate she said, I am going to send some energy before the healing session. Healing session I asked, what's that? The woman explained that most nights there were healing sessions or spiritual sessions. I was certainly more interested in these than the Sunday Service. As the woman was turning away to walk off, she said, "Of course there is the closed circle on Friday nights for people who want to train as psychic mediums". I was certainly interested in this, I asked the woman how I could join this event. The woman looked at me and laughed, "you will have to be invited she said, invited by Joe, he runs the night, and he doesn't let just anyone in," she said. I asked for Joe's telephone number and within a few minutes Joe's number was written down on a scrap of paper and given to me.

I held on to that scrap of paper for two weeks, until i built up the confidence to call Joe. Joe was a straight talker, he told me on the telephone that I would need to come to the Church on the Thursday of the next week during the healing event, Joe would need to interview me to see whether I was the right type to join the Friday night group.

I was extremely nervous, I felt very tense but wanted to meet Joe and share my experiences to see what Joe thought.

I was met by Joe at the door to the Church and taken to a side room. Joe asked me to tell him what had happened to me to make me want to join a closed spiritualist group. I felt a release, it was the first opportunity I'd had to talk about some of my experiences and I flooded with information. Joe sat listening and looked quite uninterested, he stopped me mid flow and said, "OK, your stories are interesting and you can join our group." Joe stood up abruptly and said, "see you tomorrow, 7pm, don't be late as we lock the doors at 7."

I stood up, said thank you and left. I was shocked at how Joe had brushed off my stories as though they were just normal. The people at the Friday circle must also be having some very interesting experiences I thought.

The night after, I attended the Friday night closed group, I was on time and was welcomed by Joe. "Come in and meet everyone" Joe said warmly. I had a positive feeling about this group, I was certainly the youngest there, but I was keen to meet others similar to myself. Joe was well known in the spiritualist community, he had been an active spiritual medium for many years and gave private readings on a regular basis. I spent the next 2 years regularly attending the Friday night group. Some people came and some left, it was an eclectic group of individuals from all walks of life. Some were spiritual, some spoke about connection to spirit guides and some worked with energy, angel cards, tarot cards and psychic artists. Joe was the anchor and he always had new perspectives to discuss.

I had become an integral part of the group, I was aware that my experiences were not the same as others, no one in the group had anything similar happen to them. The majority were just looking for connection.

On one of these Friday nights I attended the closed group and the room had been set out differently to the usual semi-circle. 3 chairs were positioned in the centre of the room, two chairs facing the other one. Joe asked everyone to take a seat, the seats were arranged at the back of the room, positioned so everyone could see the centre chair.

Joe said, we are going to have an exorcism, everyone looked shocked, including me, this had certainly not happened before, Joe was serious and he asked again for everyone to take a seat. All 20 group members took their seats including me, all sat quietly and watching Joes every move. He asked one of the group to move forward, she did and he said that she would be his energy and spiritual anchor whilst he performed the exorcism. She was an energy worker, a Reiki Master and Joe asked her to keep an energy link flowing towards him throughout the exorcism. She appeared to know what he was talking about, she sat calmly and held her arms forward toward Joe who was sat a few feet away. Five minutes past and one more of the group was invited to move forward. She was a younger woman, in her 30's. Joe asked her to sit on the centre chair and turned to the group. Mary has picked up a dark energy, this energy is attached to her and we are going to remove it Joe said in a matter of fact way. It is a troubled spirit, a lower form of spirit he explained. I want you all to shield yourselves with a protective energy he said and whatever you do, do not link yourselves in to this energy. I was understandably fascinated, what had attached itself to this woman? was it the same as what had attacked me some years earlier. It must be bad I thought, watching and listening intently as Joe spoke and started to work. We are going to build up a high level of energy Joe said, I am then going to focus the energy towards the spirit that is attached and free her from it. Joe started and he spoke to the spirit, his words quietened but he continued to speak. Mary began to feel uncomfortable, she moved backwards and forwards as Joe spoke, Joes intensity increased, Mary's motions backwards and forwards had increased, Mary started to wail, she was clearly in distress, I was shocked and totally transfixed on what was happening in front of me. Within a few minutes Joe was standing and had his hands close to Mary's head, she was writhing around, slurring words that did not mean anything, Joe was chanting and his energy anchor was leant forward seemingly struggling to hold Joe in place. I couldn't quite believe what I was seeing, was this made up I kept thinking, the dread of doubt filled me, was the past two years real, I felt very uncomfortable, I knew what I had experienced but this was like a horror movie playing out.

I had lost focus for a moment as I questioned myself and what was now playing out before me, as I looked up towards Joe and the scene, to refocus on the events that were unfolding in front of me, I saw it, the entity, it was real, it was there, attached to Mary's back, a large baboon looking creature, I looked away and looked back to refocus, not believing what I was seeing. It was still there, it sat upright on Mary's back with its forearms stretched out and its head stretched back as though it was pulling away from Mary. Joe continued, Mary moved backwards and forwards and I watched intently. The creature was not being pushed off by Joe, it was trying to escape, every time Joe went closer to Mary and his voice intensified the creature pushed backwards, Joe was not fighting the creature, he was fighting Mary. I watched in amazement as Joe fought and the creature fought and Mary jerked backwards and forwards wailing. Joe was now hunched over Mary, he was almost touching the creature and was chanting intently. Finally the creature's forearms were released and it reeled backwards, Joe made a surge forward and pushed the air in front of the creature, it had broken free and made a swift exit through the solid wall at the back of the room. I sat in shock, I had seen the creature, it had been trapped by Mary, she had trapped it and Joes exorcism was to save the creature from Mary, not to save Mary. As soon as the creature had become free Joe slumped in to the chair and wiped the sweat from his brow, Mary was sat upright. Staring at Joe, with a look of normality on her face. Joe looked up and his eyes met mine. Joe knew that I had seen something, it was written all over my shocked face. Joe looked at the group and nodded in appreciation of their involvement. The group were stunned and quiet, gesturing back at Joe, unsure whether to clap, cheer or stay silent.

Joe stood up and moved quickly over to me, "What did you see then'? he asked quietly. I felt very uncomfortable as what I had seen was not what I had expected and maybe not what Joe was expecting me to say. I nervously explained in detail the creature, its position and its movements as Joe was performing the exorcism, "And?" Joe asked, staring directly in to my eyes. I explained that I had seen the creature struggle and that it was Mary who had trapped it, "You released it Joe, and saved it from Mary." Joe smiled, touching my arm, "excellent," Joe said, "Mary is a troubled soul, she attracts lower spirits and then traps them in her energy field. It isn't the first and will not be the last." Joe sighed and turned back to the group to speak to them about the process of exorcism.

I was still shocked and troubled by what I had experienced, how shocking that spirits could get stuck, and humans were actually the problem, very different to the movies I had thought.

I reflected back on my experiences and thought about the dark space in my mind's eye, the space between us and everything else. The space was to protect them as much as it was to protect us.

I continued to meet up with Joe and the group for a further year until Joe retired from the group due to ill health, I continued on and off with the group for a few months after Joe had left and finally ended my time with the Friday night group soon after.

5 THE NEAR MISS

Standard days with standard daily bread,

Our light hiding under a bushel of modern day society,

And our reason for life, our development,

Halted to go no further and with no core,

No richness, no absolute

Shadowed and blind beneath the weight of history

And modern day culture.

I was now 21 years old, and had visited my Grandma and Grandad with my girlfriend. My grandparents lived an hour's drive from home and we visited them every few months for a catch up. My Grandma baked cakes without fail every week, and I always looked forward to a sticky slice of homemade Parkin when we visited. Following our visit we were driving home and had approximately 20 minutes left of the journey. It was a Saturday afternoon and the road was busy, the speed limit was 30 miles per hour and the traffic was light enough to keep a steady speed of 30 mph, the weather was warm and white wispy clouds dotted the sky. I was driving and daydreaming, suddenly, without warning a figure appeared at the front of the car, it was male and it looked as though it was sat on the bonnet with his legs disappearing towards the front of the car in between the headlights. I turned away for a moment and looked back expecting to see that the figure had disappeared. He was still there, his figure shone like iridescent light that pulsated and fluxed, shimmering and dancing in the sunlight. His face was turned towards me, and he stared directly at me with piercing white electrified eyes. I pushed my body back in to the car seat, which creaked as I pushed against the steering wheel, tensing my body and muscles, I automatically slowed the car and dropped the speed to approximately 15 mph. I tried to stop the car, releasing my foot from the accelerator, but my foot would not move away from the position it was in and I was not able to stop. The traffic was still free-flowing and a large gap quickly grew in front of the car between us and the next car in front. As both sides of the road were busy the cars behind were unable to over-take and within a few seconds I was being flashed by headlights and beeped by car horns. The figure stared at me with a concerned look and moved forward on the bonnet towards the windscreen. I pushed back harder in my seat and slowed the car down even further, my girlfriend was frantic, what are you doing she shouted, what's going on? I explained that something was happening and I was not able to speed up. I think at that point she believed that something mechanical had gone wrong with the car, which was probably for the best. The figure stared intently, and his eyes burned in to me, seemingly signifying the seriousness of the situation, and the need for me to continue to drive at a very slow and careful pace. A welcomed break in the traffic allowed cars to pass and again more beeping of horns, angry faces and hand gestures came my way. I continued at a slow pace for 3 miles, not able to stop and not able to speed up, just continuing at a steady 15mph. The figure stared intently and I stared back, there seemed no end to this situation.

As we reached the main roundabout junction close to the City, I was finally able to stop the car as my foot would now lift off fully from the accelerator. I stopped at the broken white lines that were painted on the road at the entrance to the junction. There was no need to stop at the junction as no cars were coming, the road was clear, but the figure on the bonnet had somehow now pushed down on the brake pedal and was holding us there. As I looked left again, a flash of red appeared, a Ford Fiesta, out of control and moving fast. The car was now sideways, screeched and sliding at speed towards the roundabout, it all happened so fast, I had no time to think or react. A sinister shudder ran down my spine as the Ford Fiesta hit the central mound on the roundabout, kicking up a cloud of dust and flipped over, rolling once and skidding across the road and down the embankment. As I refocused towards the figure on the bonnet my foot raised from the brake pedal and my accelerator was pressed as we entered the junction. The figure was calm, his eyes were not burning or glowing white now and his position had changed into an almost relaxed pose. I was bothered and concerned for the people in the Ford Fiesta but the figure gestured to me, pointing forwards towards the exit. He expressed a feeling on me, that all was now well, for us and for the other people in the Ford Fiesta. As I drove slowly forwards and round the roundabout I looked over to the red Ford Fiesta and the 3 occupants who were climbing out, thankfully all seemed OK. As I looked back at the figure on the bonnet he smiled, his smile grew, filling the car with bright white light until for an instance I could not see him at all. As the white light diminished, it was clear that the figure had left, the bright light disappeared and normality returned.

I reflected greatly on this event and the potential consequences that may have unfolded. In the days that followed I sought out further reading of other people that had experienced moments of danger and were profoundly saved by spiritual forces. I now believe that if I had not slowed down the car and taken the preventative measures that had been enforced by the spiritual being, we would have been hit hard by the Ford Fiesta and at least one of us, if not both of us would have been killed or at least seriously hurt that day. The figure I believe was a guardian angel and for some reason a potential future catastrophic event was to be averted and we were to be saved in that very moment. I was not told by any spiritual voice that this was a guardian angel and I had no reason to think or feel this at the time, my subsequent reading and other spiritual experiences later in life have confirmed that this was what we would consider to be a guardian angel and I felt significantly blessed that this was our day to be saved.

My additional reflections and thoughts following the near miss were focused on what we believe to be and experience as the past, the present and the future. This is clearly not the same for spirit, they fully knew that a close future event would potentially cause harm and they had decided to intervene to avert this accident. As I have mentioned, once the guardian angel appeared I was not able to stop the car, nor could I speed up, the journey had to continue and I was only allowed to slow down just enough to ensure that the close future accident did not happen, and only seconds were in play to avert the disaster. This convergence and crossing over of potential outcomes, timelines was averted through spiritual intervention, with a dramatic change of events, brought about by a minor adjustment to the speed and timing of a journey.

As my life has progressed I have come to cherish and value this experience for many reasons, taking every day since this event as a special and wonderful addition to my life, days that so very easily may not have been provided if the guardian angel had not intervened that day.

THE COSMIC GARDENER

6 THE OTHER SIDE

More open hands like flowers grow,

Together side by side,

The winds of change will propagate,

Until with all the days and nights the seed will show.

Assist the furrow and break the chain of righteousness,

For pain insist the flow of passage.

See through complex and web we weave,

To hide the real ascend.

I was now 30 years old, I was married, and owned my first house. It was a Sunday morning and I was driving towards our local American dinner for breakfast. The sun was shining and the radio was playing, the dinner was two minutes away and I was thinking about what I would order when we arrived. Within a moment and without warning a rush of energy surged in to me from the back, vibrating through my physical body and surging out of my chest, causing me to catch my breath. As the energy pushed outward I felt light pressure on my face as though two hands had been placed over my eyes, forehead and nose, similar to when children hide their eyes when playing hide and seek. As the hands were released my vision was disrupted, I can only describe it as being similar to when a person swims in the sea wearing a divers face mask. As the person slowly raises their head from the water they are able to see two places simultaneously. When the swimmer raises their head half out of the water they are able to look up to the sky, look forward to the beach and dry land, and look down beneath the water line to the sea floor and into the water surrounding them, a split view as it were, except that this was not the sea and I was not wearing a divers mask. I could see the road, I could see the car, everything that was physically in my field of vision up to point where the horizon joins the sky. Above this I could see a white glowing space, a spirit plane, a place with what looked like shimmering silver grey people moving around, similar in some way to what you would see on a busy shopping day in any local town. As I drove and finally reached the carpark of the American Dinner, I could see more spirit people, they seemed to be walking and moving around, conversing, and socialising it looked like. As they moved around I noticed some of them instantaneously shooting up out of view, leaving the space and disappearing. Whilst others would come down from another space that was out of view and join the space. I could not hear their words but could hear their muffled communication and conversations. The split view continued as I walked across the carpark and entered the dinner, I ordered breakfast and I sat down by the window to eat. I was able to function quite normally and continue to communicate with my two sons who were with me, one 5 years old and the other 2 years old. As we started to eat breakfast I looked out of the window toward the nearest town contemplating the current events that were unfolding. Again without warning and within an instant my spiritual being was pushed from my body and I was transported to the furthest point to which my eyes were fixed. Instantly I came racing back and in to my body. I looked again to a different point in the distance and instantly I was transported there out of my body and back again. The movement was so quick, I felt the rush and the speed but nothing was holding me back, no physical to slow me down, it was exhilarating beyond understanding, the speed of each trip was so quick it defied time and relativity. I felt a chord connection between my spiritual being and physical that pulled me back every time. I did this several times whilst we ate, still being able to view the spirit people in the white space as I was pulled back in to my body. We finished breakfast and we left the Dinner and I drove for 25 minutes to the sea front. The split view did not change or diminish, and I was able to view the spirit people for the entire journey. As I parked at the sea front I noticed that the white space had moved slightly in to the distance, and it was not as clear as it had been earlier. We left the car and walked to the sea front. I stopped at the railings at the sea defences, feeling the cool breeze being pushed in from the sea. I looked out across the horizon towards the distant oil platform and again I left my body and was quickly standing on the oil platform holding the safety rail. I stood there momentarily before again being pulled back and returning to my body. The freedom and exhilaration that this out of body experience gave was so sublime, unfettered and vey special. I could feel the speed of movement from one point to the other although this was not physical, I could also feel the ground beneath my feet when I stood on the platform, I could also feel the cold of the steel railing on the oil platform and the sharp cold wind as it blew across the platform. After 5 of these out of body trips to the oil platform my spirit was re-anchored to my physical being and I was unable to move out again. We slowly walked back to the car and I sat in the driver's seat watching as the white space and spirit people slowly moved away and eventually evaporated until my view was not split any longer and was only of the physical realm. As I drove back towards home I felt a spiritual presence an entity who had brought further communication and understanding. They had wanted to give me the opportunity to see the spirit realm, to understand how close it actually was to the physical realm, and how spirit could move freely from one place to another in the physical realm and the spirit realm without the physical body slowing down their movements.

This experience was the longest spiritual connection and experience that I had had up to that point in time and was another significant moment and teaching on my life's path.

7 THE ECHO FROM SPIRIT

The following chapter continues on from the poetic versus
that are included in some of the earlier chapters, and is
dedicated to a further 18 separate but connected pieces of
communication, derived from spiritual sources and
produced through a blended form of automatic writing
and spiritual connection.

THE COSMIC GARDENER

STAND FORTH

Stand and be counted without your name,

Remember that one is who and what,

Not why.

Spring from the depth of your hole,

Into the light,

With grace and harmony take flight,

Through time spent we make our life.

Portray our loyalties to book and to note,

With special conviction we provide our real,

And hold the truth, as spoken in word,

With all that we have, is not what we need.

Stand forth, without the need of man,

Nor special pride.

You are the seed of all that was,

And what will come, will have no end with time.

From ground fall short the deed will take, complete,

And utter the words no more,

REMEMBERING

Remembering our true path, Is,

Without consequence, a real issue,

And one that stands the testament of time.

Our lives have been fraught, with religion,

And societal regurgitation,

Of what we have, and what we want,

What we should be, and how we should be doing it.

Life is without doubt, a complex mode of rules,

Regulations,

Hypothetical reasons of for and against,

And with real and unreal fabrications of the truth.

RESTORE, RESTORE

From here to there the vastness shouts,

And calls the echo in,

Remove the bands of time,

And fold the space with block and bow,

Mean arc,

For restore the faith in men complete,

The cycle,

Accept the wave of Bendix draw.

PROCLAIM

Portray complete and hold no more,

For all is with us now,

Through reign we draw acceptance bound,

Stand firm without distain,

Call forth the march of all,

To look again through standard,

Bolts of horse and mane.

Strong words to truth are wrongly sworn,

Stand, repeat, proclaim,

Upheld and decreed.

THE FLAME

Beware for man without the sword,

As he is tasked with many,

The flame,

The right foreshown,

He writes the wrongs and tells a tale,

His lance is sharp and swift,

Call not to him with all your heart,

As peace is thrown too many.

AVALON

Recall the dream of dreams,

And because the need will bend and break,

Through all with clear process,

Will cut the cord of Avalon,

Complete without duress.

ALOUD AND TRUE

Uphold and store to cost again,

Before aloud and true,

The mark of man has torn beneath,

More to take,

Accept, remove and strip,

Behold the new.

Form out spin to your need,

And new,

With wing and prayer the dawn,

The mark of time, the light,

Again the tide,

THE COSMIC GARDENER

The strength of all will take its toll,

From low to high with great and bold,

The straw will break,

It holds with might its grip defiant,

With steely gaze,

The voice concern.

It tears and rips through stone and flesh,

Request upon the day,

The hill, the ceremony,

Testament, request.

MAKE A STAND

Stand for you,

For five and ten,

Together raise the port is said,

Ask foretold, for all will know,

The many faces cannot turn,

Until many turns are navigated.

A cross of old to end complete,

To reckon forth and might,

Come speed with harm to stop the flow.

The day today for old and new,

To warrant many,

Place the heart to centrefold,

THE COSMIC GARDENER

Out with care as queen,

Give time and recompense,

Move more with tone,

Forgo resist allow.

Recall the voice of onyx,

Through I and claim to throne,

Accrue the stony ground,

kindle the home fire and group,

Recall again the sign of David.

THE WHEEL

Guard the worlds from within,

For peace the wheel turns,

Your wait consigned to future

Past hope and guide,

So come the fortress,

Beneath the grind,

The depth of hue forged inside.

Remake, restore

Rebuild not straight, nor shorn,

Part in part out,

Surround.

FUTURES WELL

Above beyond, high freedom speaks,

Just hold and go to Qarta.

Mane, Jump, kick,

Ride out,

amidst deep hole and fiord,

Across border, boundary and stick.

Quest alone for futures well,

Stride out rely on journeys end,

Forego star pose, bereft of day,

For world, for all,

For unique.

THE STORM TRUE

Rune is black, repeat its trick,

Revolve, turn head and stone.

Vanquish, contain,

Through bite decroix,

Fold neat, pick up,

Leave clear, even stable.

Beat frog and toad to gate,

Through many holes and passageways,

Raise up to light,

And merge junta le costa,

Uphold the many, provide the storm true.

TOO MANY KINGS

Recover today record adrift,

Too many kings gorge fruitful, and with stain.

High blood repeat,

Down steep,

Without follow or course, for old and new,

Deed poses and keep, remain.

Uphold, sustain, be calm,

And strewn with ash, and cult,

Soar quiet, and light, fro codex bore,

Insight compress,

Benign vow, less number mean.

JUST AND COMPLETE

Many moments of time have been blessed,

And given deity through word and speech,

From man to lesser and more than,

Through free, we are locked and bound,

God saved and blessed to kiss the crown.

We are one with all,

No high, no low,

No regal gown of gold and lace,

Sign not to man nor structures make,

To keep your separate state.

THE COSMIC GARDENER

Assign with haste to your own grace,

Bring forth the know and humanity of all,

To test to time,

No war, no hate, no need, no want, just and complete.

One for all and all not one,

Together unite and keep,

Above the sound of voice and hurl,

Poetry recite through word and through song,

Bring forth the true self.

Peel back to core and build back no more,

No hidden place.

NOT ALL, BUT MANY

De-rest fortune regard and stall,

Climb hope and brawl to fin and sway.

Not all but many to keep control,

To pick and pike, calm down and out,

To ford stone and beacon.

From wed and great steeple,

By water anoint, grey stone and sept,

Behold the great partner.

End all,

Slave none,

Send the director.

RISE OUT, RISE ALL

Formation and blind gather the great seed,

Their will and testimony rigid and cold,

To stand for each other, and not for the all,

Deprived and rejected rise out,

Rise all.

Amid the blue wisps true of scent delicate,

For new beginnings brought forth,

With fine moment and threads of shine,

The hewn face of man grows tall like shadow from light,

His soul to keep, his heart to know,

The true depth of it all.

THE LOST AND FOUND

Hide, the facets of truth are masked with life,

For old and for young, No guide.

The lost and found, no difference to see,

Expectant, and waiting,

They hang from the tree.

Note tribute and foot note,

For they are the key,

Too many horde nations continue to be.

Fox wily with words, the noose tightens with haste,

Clear conscience and foresight, accept and decree.

THE GREAT DIVIDE

Precious rays of celestial light,

The rainbow ends,

The crown of ruby red.

Glide dreams of day, and dreams of night,

For crystal mine.

Her dress flows white,

Her own true fortunes told,

Blissful and sublime.

Across the great divide her feet to tread,

To mark the day for man.

ETERNAL GRACE

Waters cold and deep,

Go hundreds through wake and sleep,

Cry silent eternal grace.

Days turn though great,

The tempest quake,

Flat line.

Revolve the high,

The low,

The freeze,

And the slow.

REMAIN ETERNAL

Strings tight and pressed, remain afore,

To dent a heart through flow,

Remain eternal,

Grow deed and reason

High to end and to sound.

Accord, group jump to pour,

Without regulate and scent,

To know train,

No free and kind,

Too kind, rotate and spin,

Gross end.

8 THE JUMP

See clear, judge none for all and for one,

The threads wind tight and strong,

Yield and build before light of dawn,

Resist not what is your right to hold,

Embrace, grow wings of gold.

Sense high and low,

Free mantle grow, return your real trait.

I am going to jump to the present day for this chapter, as I need to share some information with those who have read this story thus far and shared some of the wonderful experiences that I have had. At the point of writing I have spent 50 years on this beautiful awe inspiring earth, experiencing some of the most amazing and profound spiritual events that anyone could dream of or hope for. I feel so privileged and honoured to be here, to of experienced such amazing events and life changing moments, and finally to be sharing this story with whomever cares to read it and hopefully, share it with others who may find connection with it. The significance of this journey is that this written account is not particularly about my journey, I wanted to share some of my life's experiences with you to hopefully frame the next few chapters for you.

This book was purposefully written to provide an understanding about one question, a question that I did not ask, but one that was answered through a message, a sublime message of hope and of humanity, sent from and through spiritual connection to here, an understanding, a simple and beautiful truth, the question of our existence and the reason for it, life as we know it, our short but divine reality. We are the cosmic gardeners. The reason why we are here, the reason why we do what we do, and why we think and feel as we do. The very reason for human existence, and our very special place in the Universe.

Intertwined within this wonderful message is the reason for religion, the reason for special and amazing messengers from God that have passed on knowledge and shaped and reshaped our world and finally the reason for our special relationship with God.

I had a wonderful and dramatic experience approximately 10 years ago, one that concluded the spiritual teachings that had been brought to me throughout my life. This special and profound journey started in France, continued through Spain and ended in France, it set out as a family vacation to visit relatives in Spain but turned in to the most wonderful days of my life, a journey through 2 countries and a glimpse of our human co-existence with our spiritual being.

I did not set out for a spiritual awakening, nor did I ever set out to share any of these experiences with you or anyone else, it just is what it is.

However, I do now feel that it is time to share this message with whomever cares to read it as it is too special to keep to myself and needs to be communicated. It is based only on my personal journey, and my understanding, it is a human's version of what has been shared from spirit, and based on this, I ask that you take it in the spirit that it was given, as a truth, my truth, do with it what you will, process it and reflect on it, cast it aside or take it on board. It is only one potential in the kaleidoscope of potentials, one grain of sand on all the beaches in the world. It is of value to me alone and to those that the message connects with and this message crystallizes my understanding of our co-existence with God and our spiritual journey.

Finally, I would add that the name 'Cosmic Gardener' was clearly placed by spirit communication as our central role, this title was not invented by me, it was placed firmly with me by spirit. We are Cosmic Gardeners.

9 THE JOURNEY PART 1

My journey started as a family vacation in the UK, setting off for Spain in a large motorhome with my 2 children. The plan was to visit my uncle and aunt who lived in Southern Spain, driving through France and Spain, staying with my uncle for 6 days and then returning to the UK. Our trip was underway and we had booked a ferry to France from Dover port. My plan was to drive on minor roads and not to use the motorway/ peage, this would allow us to see more of the countryside and enjoy local French and Spanish cuisine and site seeing. I had set up a large TV and games console for my two boys in the back of the motorhome, I knew it would be a long journey and the games console would be a big help as I drove for long hours. We had driven through France and had reached the Spanish border, the temperature was getting hotter and the landscape was changing from leafy greens to burnt browns and yellow. We passed through the border and continued our journey. I had set the satnav to avoid motorways and so we were frequently taken down minor roads that were becoming more and more remote. We had driven in to Spain and were crossing parts of the Pyrenees, the boys were happily playing on their console and I was driving, enjoying the scenery and quiet roads, the sun was high in the clear sky, visibility was good and the road was twisty and void of other vehicles. To the left and right were trees and shrubs, typical Spanish countryside.

There was no warning or energy surge, no subtlety and no spiritual communication, the beginning of the spiritual connection was sudden and dramatic. A figure had appeared to right of me, it was a woman, dressed in a nun's habit. She was stood at the corner of where the road turned to the left. I was almost upon her and my body tensed as I came to my senses, slowing the motorhome down significantly to ensure we were not a danger. I focused on the road and surrounding area almost expecting to see other people dressed the same or at least a vehicle, church, or houses. I quickly looked right again towards the woman who had been looking down towards the ground, as she raised her head her face became fully visible. Her face was tightly held within her veil, she stared at me, her eyes were streaming with blood, and the blood was running down her habit and forming a pool on the ground. As I reeled back in to my seat at the shock of what I was seeing, she raised off the ground and her body lunged forward toward the motorhome window. I stamped on the brakes and came to a screeching halt. The woman was now millimeters from the side window and I could see her full face, her eyes were not visible as blood was flowing through her eye sockets. Her face was distorted with pain and anguish, and the site was truly horrific. She stayed visible for a few seconds at the window, a spiritual force exploded from her and pushed through the motorhome. It was a spiritual copy of her, what I would describe as a ghostly apparition, what you would typically see on a well-made horror movie. It pushed up in to my physical and I felt deep pain, anguish, a flood of negative emotion and a seismic horror, that vibrated far in to the distance, bringing floods of excruciating raging sadness.

Within seconds I was back to the motorhome, the woman had gone and the connection had gone with her. I pulled off the road, jumped out of the motorhome and fell to my knees, sobbing and grinding my teeth with the overwhelming emotion that was riding up from my spiritual being. I struggled to stand, holding my chest tightly as the emotion flooded from me. I looked round, half expecting to see the woman again, but she had gone. I staggered up the road and back again, I struggled to steady myself and crouched down, bending my knees until I could touch the ground with my hands. I grabbed at the dry earth and squeezed handfuls of it in to my fists. Small sharp stones dug in to my hands and the sharpness caused a stabbing pain. This pain was relieving my inner pain and I tightened my grip to intensify the feeling. I raised myself up and to my feet, looking up towards the sky and shouted. I had no words, I could only wail, and cry. I walked up and down again, trying to manage my feelings, I was now bothered about the boys who luckily were still engrossed in their console game.

I quickly put my sunglasses on, covering my swollen bloodshot eyes, and slumped in to the driver's seat of the motorhome. I turned to the boys and with a shaky voice I said, 'all good' and restarted the engine. The boys didn't even look up from their game and didn't respond. I breathed deeply and slowly drove away.

The image of the woman's face was burned in to my minds eye and I was frantically trying to make sense of the experience as I drove on. The scenery changed as we made our way further in to Spain, and had become mountainous and thick with tress.

An hour or so had passed, and I had driven steadily up a steep road through the trees, as the road levelled out and then started to drop the road angled left and became quite steep. At the side of the road to the right, the terrain fell away into a small valley, and as I started to descend, a small round/ octagonal church type building came in to view, approximately 200 to 300 yards away. I could see the top of the building, and above the pitched roof approximately 5 feet higher, I could see a silver glowing web that stretched out covering the building. The web was the shape of a spider's web and shafts of white glowing light shone down from the sky through the intersections of the web and into the building through the roof. I eased off the accelerator and moved my foot across to press the brake. I was abruptly told not to stop and just to view the angelic light that was being drawn in to the building. I watched wide eyed, straining my neck to see, until I had driven too far down the road to view the web or the building. I tried to catch a further view in my large side mirrors, but the exterior stone wall was blocking the view.

I continued my journey in to Spain and the following day I had reached my destination, arriving at my uncle's villa.

10 THE VACATION

We had finally arrived at my uncle's villa and I took some time to walk in the adjacent nature reserve to reflect on the recent experiences. As I walked I felt a warm comfort and acceptance of what I had experienced, there was a spiritual connection with me that was calming my physical, my spiritual and soul. I savored these moments as I connected with the natural surroundings, and I slowly walked back towards my uncle's villa. That night we sat on the balcony of the villa and ate food that my aunt had prepared for us, we chatted and caught up on life and drank Spanish red wine. Later that evening my uncle told me about one of his English neighbors, who ran a local church and seemed to be spiritual. My uncle connected with this person and was keen for me to meet with her. My uncle had an understanding that I'd had some spiritual experiences in my life but was not aware of the detail, but he thought it was a good idea for me to meet with her.

I agreed and the following day my uncle had arranged for us to spend some time with his friend. We walked for a few minutes and stood outside a small, simple looking Spanish house. He knocked on the door and we were greeted by a short older woman who clearly had a mobility problem and was uneasy on her feet. We were invited in and we sat in the small front sitting room. My uncle introduced me and seemed quite nervous. The woman stared at me, and smiled, she told me that she had been asked by spirit to set up a local church group and had done what she had been asked. It was part of her spiritual journey and she was enjoying the experience. Her tone was assured and she was calm and confident, she talked about her ailments and her husband's medical issues, she had no complaints and wasn't moaning, she was quite matter of fact and wanted me to know that even though they both had issues she was still carrying out want she had been asked to do by spirit. My uncle sat silently listening to her, he clearly respected her, and revered her position and spiritual calling. As she spoke she briefly described a spiritual space, calling it a 'White Hall'. My spine tingled and my eyes widened. I interrupted and asked her to repeat what she had said. "Did you just mention a White Hall?" I asked. "Yes," she quickly replied, her eyes narrowed as she focused on my face, "Why," she asked. "Well," I replied, "I had a spiritual experience a few years back and was taken to a White Hall," she clapped and smiled, "You too," she said with an excitement in her voice. My uncle started to look confused, and wasn't quite sure what was now happening.

"How did it start for you," she quickly asked. "Well," I nervously replied, "This is going to sound weird," I exclaimed. "I woke up one morning and saw a spiraling white cloud above my head in the shape of a wide funnel, approximately 6 feet in diameter." "And the black one" she quickly asked. I stuttered and stopped talking for a moment, my uncle jerked back in to his seat. I leaned forward, "Yes" I said "and then the black one came from beneath me, rising up until it finally touched and joined with the white one." She interrupted again, "It was a white man and a black man for me." "And when they touched," her eyes widened and her face was expectant and excited. "And when they touched" I said, "I was taken up through the gateway that these two spiraling clouds had made". "In to the White Hall" she exclaimed. "Yes," I replied, "in to the White Hall." My uncle had a tear welling up in his eye, as we joined our stories and experiences in to one. The White Hall was a beautiful spiritual place, a large glowing hall of white cloud looking material where higher spiritual beings carried out some kind of function. "And what did you see?" she asked excitedly. "Well, it's a bit weird," I said again, "'part of the hall was a viewing place where the floor was not white and was transparent." "Dead people," she replied. My uncle sat up abruptly and I said "yes, a flow of thousands of spirits moving at speed like a river beneath my feet." "Yes" she said, clapping her hands excitedly, "Exactly" she exclaimed, she continued, "As people die their spirits would move out and travel past this place, being monitored by higher spiritual beings, and we have been lucky enough to see it." "Yes" I quickly replied, as we excitedly exchanged our experiences. The tears were now running down my uncle's face, he was overwhelmed by what we were describing, and the experiences that we were now sharing. As the discussion about the White Hall came to an end, she abruptly said, "Not much more to discuss here, it was lovely to meet you". She turned to my uncle who was wiping the tears from his face, and said, "He is special, thank you for bringing him to meet with me". My uncle smiled nervously and we said our goodbyes. We walked back to the villa in silence as my uncle tried to process what he had just heard. At the end of the walk he grasped my hand and thanked me for such a special experience. That night we sat on the balcony again eating food that had been prepared by my aunt and drank red wine. My boys, my uncle and aunt started to play a board game and I sat looking over the balcony deep in thought. As I looked out on to the nature reserve I had an all too familiar rush of energy push in to me, and once again my spiritual viewing space opened up. This was different as I could physically see what was in the space as though it was being projected outwards in to my field of vision. Rows of cinema seats appeared, and in front of the seats sat a high stage with heavy red velvet curtain draped down across the stage cutting off the view, as though a play was about to start.

A figure of a man appeared, sat on the front row looking towards the stage. I was automatically moved forward and sat down besides the figure. I was not able to move my head to the side and look at him, I was only able to look straight ahead, viewing the stage. The curtain drew back and the stage opened up. To the left was a large ornate Helter-Skelter slide, to the right was an old fashioned ornate Merry go Round and in front of the merry go round was a woman sat on a bicycle, stooped forward, and looking like she was moving at full speed, but she was stationary and not moving. The figure sat next to me softly spoke, "Look at the stage, what do you see?" he asked. "An old fashioned fun fair," I replied. "This is life" he replied. "The whole of human existence." The specific detail wasn't spoken, but was impressed on me, so I could fully appreciate the meaning. The Helter-Skelter represented reward for effort. People effort to climb the stairs and then are rewarded for the effort when they slide down to the bottom. Every day in life people effort for reward and so it continues. The Merry Go Round represents the journey, the feeling of movement and distance travelled, without actually getting anywhere, A continuous cycle of social conditioning, blinding the real senses, putting humans to sleep, with the belief that they are actually getting somewhere. The woman on the bicycle believes she is speeding towards her destination, efforting as hard as she can to get there. Not only will she never get there, she isn't even moving, she doesn't know that she is stationary, stuck in her intent.

The figure turned to me, "If this is what you want then get out of the chair and join them, or remain here with me in the real." I tried to turn my head again to see the man that sat by the side of me, but I was still unable to move my head. "Well, what will it be" the man said quietly but firmly. "I choose to stay here," I said, "I choose the real". "Then get off the stage" he said. I looked up and saw myself sat on the Merry Go Round, buying in to the human condition without question, without thought. I was shocked, and managed to turn my head slightly to view the man's clothing. He was wearing a vibrant yellow and brown tartan suit, a smart suit that was perfectly tailored to his frame. I still wasn't able to look at his face, and I looked back to the stage, asking, "Who are you?" The reply came quickly, but was unexpected, "Angel Michael" he said, and within a second the connection went, and I was back on the balcony with my family.

Approximately thirty minutes had passed and again the stage and the rows of seats came in to view. Again the figure, Angel Michael was sat on the front row and I was quickly brought forward and was sat next to him. Again he asked, "Is this what you want?", my reply was instant, "No" I said firmly, "No I don't". "Then get off the stage" he said again. This time I was sat on the back of the bicycle, sat behind the woman. I could feel the speed of the bicycle, I could feel the immense effort that she was putting in to cycling and the focus of her thoughts, driving her to effort so hard. I was part of her, I was also efforting, focused with intent. I also wasn't moving, I was sat frozen in time, it was all a façade. I pulled back away from the woman, I was stuck like glue to the bicycle and to the intent. "It is going to be difficult," said Angel Michael. "You will have to effort with all that you have to leave the stage." I pulled and strained, pulling myself free of the bicycle, and stepping off on to the stage. As I stepped down I was instantly taken the stairs of the Helter-Skelter. Every cell in my system pushed for me to climb and effort for reward, but I pulled back and stepped down again on to the stage floor. Instantly I was sat on the Merry Go Round, astride a horse, I could hear the music, I could feel the movement of the horse as it moved up and down and the feeling of forward movement as the Merry Go Round turned and revolved. My hands were tightly grasping the pole and felt as though they were stuck firm. I pulled and pulled until my hands were free and eventually I stepped off, back on to the stage. A slow clap came from the front row, and I was transported off the stage and back to the seat next to Angel Michael. "Every day for the rest of your time on planet earth, you will have to effort to stay off that stage," he said firmly. "These seats are cold and lonely, you will be isolated, however, you will be free from the human condition, and you will have a place from where you can view life as we do." Again I was disconnected, taken back to the balcony where my family were sat, where I sat deep in thought about this new experience.

Our visit was supposed to last for 7 days before we took the journey back to the UK, but on the 4th day firm communication came from spirit, time to leave, time to finish the journey. The Push to leave was strong, there was a wall of blackness in front of me and all around me, there was nothing here for me now and I had to go. I spoke to my uncle and indicated that I had been communicated to and told to continue our journey. He smiled and seemed to understand, his acceptance was total and he hugged me thanking me for being there. The following morning we set off back the way that we had come, making our way back to the Spanish/ French border.

11 THE JOURNEY PART 2

I waited expectantly for something, a message, another dramatic experience, but nothing came. Later that day we passed through the border in to France and continued to drive until we stopped at a campervan stop over. We slept over and woke early to continue our journey. I started to question the urgency of the return journey, why had spirit pushed so hard for us to return I pondered. We set off and soon I felt a rush of energy push through the cabin of the motorhome, again a wave of energy surged through, pulsating and vibrating, it continued and I waited for the next experience. I didn't need to wait long, a figure had appeared at the front of the motorhome, floating in midair and stood approximately 6 foot from the front window of the motorhome. It was the nun that I had seen a few days before, her face this time was filled with golden light, and she emanated a beautiful warm energy of love and kindness. She was looking directly at me and as we drove on she kept pace with the motorhome. An hour or so had passed and she was still there, floating slightly above the ground and looking in to the cabin. She then started to move closer towards the cabin until she was actually inside the cabin and only a foot or so away from me. The energy was beautiful, warm, healing and angelic. I bathed in her glow, soaking up the energy that she was pushing towards me. She slowly started to turn and moved back as though she was going to leave, her face was now facing away from me and I could only see her from the back. I smiled and relaxed with a deep sigh, and as I did so, she turned, lunging towards me with a scowling, angry, sinister face, I reeled back, tensing my body and letting out a terrified shriek. She turned again and left the cabin, resuming her position outside, keeping pace with the motorhome. I breathed heavily, shocked and shaken from the experience, and as I calmed my nerves, I felt a second entity had entered the cabin behind me to the left. I was now scared and nervous and tensed my body hunching forward towards the steering wheel, pre-empting what might happen. A wave of energy came, different to any other energy I had felt. As it passed through me my emotions exploded, tears streamed down my face, and with every wave of energy, more emotion, more tears. The figure had moved closer and was within a few inches of my face. I turned and stared in to the man's warm eyes, he smiled at me with an angelic knowing smile. "It's all ok," he quietly whispered, looking forward towards the road and gesturing with his hand for us to continue the journey. His energy was deep and sublime, I had no need to ask him who he was, I already knew who he was, this was Jesus, and his physical features were exactly as you would know him from the artists impressions from the bible and other religious works of art. I couldn't believe that this was happening to me, in France and whilst I was driving a motorhome with my two children sat in the back playing console games.

He didn't say anything, his energy was enough. I bathed in his light and surrendered to the experience. I had noticed that the nun had now repositioned herself and was now in front of the motorhome to the centre, guiding our journey from her position, approximately 10 feet in front.

A few hours passed and I had to stop for food and gas, the boys had become restless and wanted a change of scenery. We finally stopped at a campervan stop over and bizarrely, I left the motorhome and our two companions to walk to the local shops for provisions. When we returned our companions had gone, I felt deflated and guilty for leaving, but I had to attend to the boys and ensure that they were OK and happy. That night I woke up abruptly, aware of a presence in the motorhome, the boys were fast asleep and I quietly asked who it was and what they wanted. A whisper came through the darkness, my body tensed and a shiver ran down my spine, "We have brought you a message, a final understanding," the voice said. "The meaning of human existence," the voice continued, "The reason why you were created and why you are all so special". "Cosmic Gardeners, this is what you are, Cosmic Gardeners, one family, one purpose, to bring consciousness to the unconscious." The voice went silent and I slumped back on to the bed falling in to a deep sleep. I awoke again some time later feeling a presence again, this was different, and this time a vision came, a star gate alignment was impressed upon me, one that will happen sometime in the near future, allowing spirit to exit this galaxy and this earthly realm and enter other galaxies that have habitable planets. Again, I slumped back on to the bed falling in to deep sleep.

When I woke in the morning the experience was burned in to my consciousness, the voice, the words, the meaning of life.

Our journey continued and we drove through France making our way further north towards home. The roads were quite clear of other traffic, the sun was shining and I hoped that there was more connections to come. Again the nun appeared in front of the motorhome and within seconds Jesus was again sat close to my left shoulder. I felt so alive, such an amazing feeling, I vocalized, thanking God and putting my hands together to rejoice. Jesus turned to me with an excited face, smiling and pointing towards the horizon, "It's here," he said, "you will see," he grinned from ear to ear, pointing and gesturing excitedly. I looked beyond the trees to the horizon but saw nothing. He gestured again as though I had missed what he was pointing at, "They built this for me." I stared and looked but only saw trees and the road ahead. "You will see" he said excitedly. I drove for approximately 40 minutes, seeing nothing but trees. The nun was still there, guiding us forward, and he was now stood up pointing and gesturing more and more. The road climbed slightly and as we got closer to the peak of the hill, I saw it, what looked like a tower came in to view, "I can see it" I said excitedly, "'wait," he said, "wait and see," "This is where I come to spend time, it is special." As we reached the top of the hill the building was becoming more and more clear. A large Cathedral type building was appearing in the distance. The satnav pointed straight and he gestured to turn off. I did and was soon driving on the narrow streets of Beauvais. It was Beauvais Cathedral, a place that he frequented, such a beautiful building I thought. I drove close to the Catheral and was looking desperately for a place to stop so I could visit this amazing place. "No," he firmly said, "Don't stop, carry on, don't stop." I carried on, and asked why he didn't want me to stop. He said that the building was built with great faith, courage and sacrifice, he came here to honour the people who had built the Cathedral not the building itself. It was the depth of the faith of the people that had built this building that he came for and adored. He praised them and they held a special place with him. We continued our journey out of Beauvais and further north.

Our two companions stayed with us all the way until we reached the ferry port in Calais, and as we departed for England they left our company.

12 COSMIC GARDENER

All earthly modes of men and beast will end

And call to you through the scene,

Revolving up closed and coupled together,

THE COSMIC GARDENER

Drawn from sight before the end,

The beginning,

The star struck mode

Profound, prophetic,

Resound, resound.

The physical world is certainly an interesting and thought provoking place, not to mention, beautiful, diverse and precious. It has such promise and such richness, it is as we believe, our only home, and currently the only place that we know that can sustain life. We have no means to escape it, no spaceship to take us to other planets, and even if we did have the technology to do so, our bodies are too frail to survive these types of journeys. We are bound by our physicality to live out our lives here, on mother earth, moving slowly along on the conveyor belt of life.

So, what about it then, the big question, the meaning of it all, life, what is it really all about. Why do we do what we do? Why are we here? Was it all created by some higher power? Is this part of a bigger plan? A bigger system?

The questions go on and on, and I believe that we have all asked these questions at least once in our lives.

I was also intrigued, why wouldn't I be, there must be an answer to all this, why are we here?

It is the seeker in me that asks the 'Why' question. It is the engineer in me that asks the 'How' question, and it is the dreamer that asks the 'Who' question. Is there one answer, or are there multiple answers, we know so much and yet we know so little. If we did have an answer, a defined truth, defining why we are here, our purpose, would it help? , would it change us? , would we be happy and content with the answer? Or, would we just start to look for a different question?

If we had an answer to this question, would it unite us? , would it dissolve the barriers that we have built between countries? , between colour, religion and race? Would it really matter to us? , or would we just carry on? , the blind leading the blind. Would we accept life? , accept our death? , would it really change our fundamental reason for existence?

The following pages of writings are a collection of

communications from the conscious mind, from the soul and from the spirit. They are connected whilst being separate, they are simple, whilst some are cryptic and poetic. They will hopefully spark some interest within each person who reads these words, some of this will make sense, some of it may not, and it will be for the reader to decide, for the scientist in you, for the believer in you, for the seeker, for the dreamer, for the human, to absorb the information, letting it perforate through you and in to your spiritual being.

The Cosmic Gardener is a potential, a reason, a purpose, and, it is a function, pure and simple. As Gardeners we have inbuilt programmes that drive every one of us to do what we do, it is our base instinct, our meaning, the reason we wake, the reason we reproduce and the reason why we keep doing the same things, day after day, year upon year, one purpose, one singular directive, to tend the garden (this planet) the best that we can. Keep mother earth in order, and apply consciousness to the unconscious. The planet is not ours, we are but brief custodians in time, providing a helping hand, just over 7.8 billion helping hands in reality, a collective of different peoples, but one, united in a single purpose.

The 'Cosmic' relates to the Universe and the question of

life beyond this planet. There are gardeners like us but different, tending other planets, keeping the far off habitable planets conscious, all created by a higher indescribable force that for some of us is God.

Cosmic Gardeners are conscious beings, and specifically coded to apply this consciousness, repeating the same cycle every day, every week, month and year. Applying treatment to the environment in which they live, whilst everything else that has life on the habitable planets is unconsciously existing, unwittingly and unknowingly pushing at the balance of what keeps the habitable planets habitable. If habitable planets do not have conscious beings they become unbalanced and chaotic, eventually becoming wastelands and uninhabitable.

The Cosmic Gardeners, a true family of spiritually connected, human beings, consciously existing on this planet, working together to one end, keep the planet in order, tend to the disorder, and keep the unconscious in check.

If we have code, then we have been coded, created to function, with purpose, and with reason. We have also been made aware of our lives and our brief existence, we also know that we will one day die and physically exist no longer. This, for conscious beings is one of the biggest fights, a fight that exists in our minds and in our hearts, our ultimate end is at odds with our very existence. We feel eternal as our soul and spirit are exactly that, timeless and existing without end. We are both eternal and have a shelf life, two opposing forces constantly pushing and pulling within our core, we have hope for our lives and we have determination to live, to carve out a personal but connected existence as best we can. Our deaths elude us and are hidden from view. Our death as we hope, is far off and in the distant future. For some of us this is true, for others, it is just around the corner. Our ability to not see the future, not see what happens to us, gives us hope for the now, it spurs us on and keeps us motivated, just one more day, 5 more years, constant hope and faith that we will survive.

A creator, or multiple creators who were in need of a conscious workforce, an engineered, built army of biomechanical workers, ones that are conscious but will carry out instinctual, unconsciously driven pre-coded orders. It is quite concerning that our base instinct may have been pre-programmed to bring order to chaos, building barriers, keeping order, protecting, subdividing, and containing.

THE COSMIC GARDENER

13 UNDERSTANDING OUR CODE

Become complete,

The path winds and peaks,

Together bond release deceit

And honour bound,

Gourd out divine retreat,

From dearest arms of friend and main

To roam and work so lent more to free the shone.

To understand this potential further I ask that you look around you and observe the reality in which you and I both physically exist. Just look around your home or working environment. We have built roads, walls, bridges, doors, gates, fences, hedges, and boundaries, the list is long. We build these because we have developed a modern society, culturally together but socially separated by locks and keys. This human made infrastructure cuts through the natural order, cuts through the unconscious, it applies human formulated rules to nature's consistent push against the balance, and we tend the garden, keeping order and control. Nature is not conscious, it lives without knowing, and without human intervention it would ultimately overtake itself.

As technology has advanced, our interventions have become more widespread, we are truly a global phenomena, reaching every part of the planet and applying our methods. As we increase in number our voraciousness to take more has exponentially grown, each one of us making a contribution to the demise of our only home. As we know more, and our knowledge expands, we increase our application and want more again.

Our coding is different to that of other humanoids on other habitable planets, ours is in part aggressive, and

120

destructive, it has ultimately pushed at the balance of the planet, pollution, global warming, over farming, deforestation, again the list is extensive. We have over gardened, been too efficient in our job to control and manage. Many are trying desperately to bring the balance back, trying to stop the over application of our operations, trying to reverse global warming, reduce plastics, clean the environment, etc, etc. It all seems very sensible, doesn't it? , so why is it not working? Are we not clever enough? I think we are, do we not know that we are the ones doing it? I think we do. Then why can't we stop it? Why can't we stop killing the one place that allows us to exist?

Simple answer is, our code is too strong, and we have to know what we are, before we can stop doing what we are doing. If we know that it is our code that drives us we can manage ourselves and apply technology, rules and regulation to protect ourselves from ourselves. This is not country versus country, it is us versus ourselves. We need to know what we are before we can formulate the global management of self. We are too preoccupied with the perceived difference between cultures, religions, districts and countries. Our personalised drive separates us, it's 'us and them', the privileged and less fortunate, winners and losers, the weak and the strong, you get the idea. If I think

I am on top then I am, build the wall higher, amass more, segregate and isolate. There is no stopping it unless we stop it.

Other planets have humanoids that have softer coding, and not the same as us. This has created problems in a different way. Here, nature has pushed forward and has tipped the balance, overgrown and slowly dying, the humanoids are unable to stop it, it is not in their nature, not in their base coding. The unconscious has pushed and it has overgrown, unwittingly suffocating the life from the planet.

THE COSMIC GARDENER

Proving our patronage

And asking for forgiveness,

To be taken to a higher place is with us all,

And will end with us all.

Pretend to be someone and hold that thought,

As with all thoughts there comes war,

And with war there are losers,

And losers without the winning we all desire so.

14 THE STAR GATE

Six gates, six axis,

The strand is tall,

It waits undiscovered for straight,

It holds the key and code for humanity for all,

Position relative to retain,

Remove the barrier to complete the strain.

The answer to these planetary issues is quite a simple one
and rooted in our spiritual existence. The question you
might ask at this point is why, if there is a God, has he or
she allowed this to happen? Why have they not
intervened? Well, the answer is, they have, and it will soon
be time, intervention is coming and it will initiate a
profound change. At a pre-determined point in our planets
future an inter-galactic connection will be made between
planets, this will be a spiritual highway connection that will
allow the passage of spirit between planets. It will allow
our spirits, once we die to travel through cosmic gateways
and be reborn on other planets. At the same time the
occupants of the other planet will travel here and be
reborn. Our coding intact, we will once again bring balance
back to the planet that we have been assigned, and the
process will continue until the balance becomes
unbalanced once more. This divergence will take
approximately 125 years as this is how long it takes for
every single person on this planet to pass away. We will be
replenished and we will replenish. We will not return to
this earth for thousands of years, until the inevitable
occurs again, we will build and we will control, we manage
the unconscious and we will bring life back to the planet

for which we are posted to. The same will be of this
planet, the new gardeners will allow the unconscious room
to grow and ultimately the balance will shift.

THE COSMIC GARDENER

Printed in Great Britain
by Amazon

64958591R00078